Magic, Myth, and Mys...

BIGFOOT

DO YOU BELIEVE?

This series features creatures that excite our minds. They're magical. They're mythical. They're mysterious. They're also not real. They live in our stories. They're brought to life by our imaginations. Facts about these creatures are based on folklore, legends, and beliefs. We have a rich history of believing in the impossible. But these creatures only live in fantasies and dreams. Monsters do not live under our beds. They live in our heads!

45th Parallel Press

Published in the United States of America by Cherry Lake Publishing
Ann Arbor, Michigan
www.cherrylakepublishing.com

Reading Adviser: Marla Conn MS, Ed., Literacy specialist, Read-Ability, Inc.
Book Design: Felicia Macheske

Photo Credits: © BestGreenScreen/Shutterstock.com; © hecubus/Shutterstock.com, 1; © NisianHughes/ Getty Images, 5; © Kirsanov Valeriy Vladimirovich/Shutterstock.com, 7; © RyanJLane/iStock, 8; © Catalin Petolea/Shutterstock.com, 11; © nhauscreative/iStock, 13; © Rich Legg/iStock, 15; © Hemera Technologies/ Thinkstock, 16; © Kelly vanDellen/Shutterstock.com, 18; © microgen/iStock, 21; © Tom McHugh/ Getty Images, 22; © Eon Alers/Shutterstock.com, 24; © Randy L. Rasmussen/Polaris/Newscom, 27; © GROGL/ Shutterstock.com, 29

Graphic Elements Throughout: © denniro/Shutterstock.com; © Libellule/Shutterstock.com; © sociologas/ Shutterstock.com; © paprika/Shutterstock.com; © ilolab/Shutterstock.com; © Bruce Rolff/Shutterstock.com

45th Parallel Press is an imprint of Cherry Lake Publishing.

Library of Congress Cataloging-in-Publication Data

Names: Loh-Hagan, Virginia, author.
Title: Bigfoot : magic, myth, and mystery / by Virginia Loh-Hagan.
Description: Ann Arbor : Cherry Lake Publishing, [2016] | Series: Magic, myth, and mystery | Includes bibliographical references.
Identifiers: LCCN 2016004922 | ISBN 9781634711166 (hardcover) | ISBN 9781634713146 (pbk.) | ISBN 9781634712156 (pdf) | ISBN 9781634714136 (ebook)
Subjects: LCSH: Sasquatch—Juvenile literature.
Classification: LCC QL89.2.S2 L64 2016 | DDC 001.944—dc23
LC record available at http://lccn.loc.gov/2016004922

Cherry Lake Publishing would like to acknowledge the work of The Partnership for 21st Century Skills. Please visit *www.p21.org* for more information.

Printed in the United States of America
Corporate Graphics Inc.

TABLE of CONTENTS

Hairy Giants

What are Bigfoot? What are types of Bigfoot? What do Bigfoot look like?

"Beware of hairy giants." People long ago said this about Bigfoot. Bigfoot isn't a name for one creature. It describes a type of creature. There are several hundred Bigfoot. They have big feet. That's how they got their name. Their footprints are 24 inches (61 centimeters) long. They're 8 inches (20.3 cm) wide. Their feet have thick **soles**. Soles are the bottoms of feet.

They live in forests. They live in mountains. They live all over. But they mainly live in the Pacific

Northwest. They live in California. They live in Oregon. They live in Washington.

Bigfoot *is the term used to describe one or many of these creatures.*

Explained by Science!

"Blobsquatch" is a blob in a photo or video. Some people think the blob is Bigfoot. Others think these blobs are real things. They see shadows. They see dark spots. They see tree stumps. They don't see Bigfoot. Bigfoot believers want to see Bigfoot. There's a scientific explanation for this. Some people have pareidolia. This is psychological. Their minds see or hear things that aren't there. They mostly see faces. Pareidolia causes people to interpret images, patterns, or sounds. Some think this is about protection. People see faces in things to be prepared. They want to be aware of their surroundings. They'd rather be safe than sorry!

Scientists think Bigfoot is a combination of folklore, hoax, and misidentification.

There are different types of Bigfoot. Sasquatch are similar to Bigfoot. But they live in Canada. They're active at night. They're fast runners. Some say they steal food. Some say they capture humans.

Yeti are shorter than Bigfoot. They live in the Himalayas. These are mountains in Asia. Yeti are called **Abominable** Snowmen. Abominable means horrible. Yeti come from cavemen. They have magical powers. They have loud screams.

There are others. Yowie live in Australia. Yeren live in China. Honey Island Swamp Monsters live in Louisiana.

Bigfoot are 7 to 10 feet (2 to 3 meters) tall. They're covered in dark hair. They have many muscles. They have wide shoulders. They have long arms. They have thick legs. They weigh 1,000 pounds (453.6 kilograms).

They have gorilla faces. They have large foreheads. They have a **ridge** above their eyebrows. A ridge is a bump.

Their bodies look more human. They walk on two legs. They walk **upright**. Upright means standing.

They're different from humans and apes. They're bigger. They have different **gaits**. Gaits are walking styles. Bigfoot take long steps. They swing their arms wide. They don't bounce their steps.

Bigfoot don't have claws.

Chapter Two

Beyond Big Feet

What are Bigfoot's strengths? How are Bigfoot territorial?

Bigfoot use their size. They lift heavy rocks. They lift cars. They twist tree trunks. They eat meat and plants. They kill prey. They swipe with their fists. They twist necks.

They survive in tough weather. They survive on tough land. Their feet are special. They're built to travel on rough ground.

Bigfoot have good senses. They run as fast as horses. They're powerful swimmers. They jump high.

They communicate. They make loud calls over long distances. They click. They howl. They grunt. They growl.

Bigfoot noises sound like knocking on wood.

When Fantasy Meets Reality!

Some people confuse Bigfoot with American black bears. These bears are the most common type of bears in North America. They can walk on their hind legs. They stand up to 7 feet (2 m) tall. They stand to get a better view. They stand to smell their surroundings. They're large. They have big shoulders. They're hairy. John Napier is a scientist. He studies Bigfoot. He said, "At a distance, a bear might be mistaken for a man when standing still. . . . The hind foot of the bear is remarkably human-like." These bears have Bigfoot behaviors. They eat the same foods. They visit camps. They make similar sounds. They live in the same areas.

Bigfoot react better to women and children than to men.

Bigfoot are **territorial**. They guard their space. They guard their homes. They guard their families.

They usually run away. They don't want to harm humans. They rarely attack. But they do scare humans away. They scream. They throw rocks. They shake trees. They snap branches. They thump their chests.

They may **stalk** humans. Stalk means to follow. Bigfoot track humans. They watch them. They study them. They run away before being seen.

Chapter Three

Hide and Seek

Why are Bigfoot hard to find? What are Bigfoot's weaknesses? How do they die?

Bigfoot only like other Bigfoot. They don't trust other **species**. Species are groups of living things. Bigfoot don't like attention. They stay out of sight. They do not want to be seen. That's why they're hard to find. They're hard to photograph. They're hard to film. They leave behind footprints.

Bigfoot blend in. They live in nature. They live out in the open. They build homes using plants. They move when seen. They don't stay in the same place.

Some Bigfoot groups are aggressive, but most aren't.

When scared, Bigfoot can make themselves smell worse.

But their smell gives them away. Bigfoot smell really bad. They can be found by sniffing the air. At the same time, their smell is a weapon. It keeps people far away.

Bigfoot don't have superpowers. They don't live forever. They live about 35 years. They can't heal themselves. They can be killed. They die from sicknesses. They die from living out in nature. They die from old age. Dying Bigfoot have thinning hair. They have wrinkles. They have open sores.

SURVIVAL TIPS!

- Leave the area. Don't get into Bigfoot's space.

- Leave dogs at home. Bigfoot hate dogs. They chase them. They kill them.

- Get a bright flashlight. Bigfoot don't like bright lights. They'll run away.

- Offer Bigfoot food. This distracts them. Then run away.

- Bring a shield. Bigfoot throw rocks. They throw branches.

- Don't leave raw meat outside. Lock up food.

- Respect nature. Don't make too much noise. Don't hunt too many animals. Don't destroy their natural homes.

- Run in a zigzag. Bigfoot run fast. But they run straight. They burst through trees and branches. Avoid open spaces.

- Don't directly look at them. Don't challenge Bigfoot.

Bigfoot are hard to find while living. They're also hard to find dead. They don't leave behind dead bodies. They bury their dead. They put heavy rocks over the bodies. No one has found Bigfoot **remains**. Remains are dead body parts.

Dead bodies don't last long in forests. They don't last long on mountains. Animals eat dead bodies. They eat bones. They eat hair. Other body parts get destroyed. They're taken in by nature.

Bigfoot have been spotted carrying their dead.

Some think Bigfoot came from humans. Some researchers found a link. They connected Bigfoot to Paranthropus. They lived 2.5 million years ago. They're near-humans.

Paranthropus had ridges above their eyebrows. They walked on two legs. They were less than 5 feet (1.5 m) tall. They lived in forests. They ate plants. They had strong jaws. They had strong chewing muscles. They had huge back teeth. They were nicknamed "Nutcracker Men."

Paranthropus fossils were found in Africa.

Know the Lingo!

- **Bigfooter:** someone who believes in and/or searches for Bigfoot

- **Bipedal:** walking on two legs

- **Cryptids:** creatures like Bigfoot that may or may not exist

- **Cryptozoologists:** people who hunt Bigfoot or other monsters

- **Cryptozoology:** scientific study of and search for creatures like Bigfoot

- **Encounter:** an actual meeting

- **Habitat:** an animal's home

- **Hirsute:** having or covered with hair

- **Hominid:** group made up of great apes and ancestors

- **Hominin:** group made up of humans and ancestors

- **Humanoid:** looking like a human

- **Primate:** group of animals that includes humans, apes, and monkeys

- **Scat:** animal poop

- **Skookum:** Chinook word for Bigfoot

- **Tracker:** someone who follows an animal's footprints and scat

- **Woolly:** covered with hair

There aren't many Bigfoot. But people report **sightings**. They've been doing so for many years. Sightings are people seeing Bigfoot.

Bigfoot live in small family groups. Females mix among family groups. They have babies. They keep the species alive. They mate in May and June.

Bigfoot babies are small. They're 6 feet (1.8 m) by age 10. They stay with their mothers when young. They're born about five years apart. Many babies die. It's hard having a Bigfoot baby.

People track footprints of family groups.

Chapter Five

Spooky Sightings

What are some important Bigfoot sightings?

Native Americans told stories about "hairy giants." J. W. Burns collected these stories. He did this in the 1920s. He first used the word Sasquatch.

Jerry Crew found a 16-inch (40.6 cm) footprint. This happened in 1958. It was in Bluff Creek, California. The newspapers called the creature "Bigfoot." The name stuck.

Crew's footprint was fake. His boss tricked him. But it didn't matter. The legend of Bigfoot started.

People reported sightings. They took photos. They took recordings. They collected footprints. Some evidence may be real. Some were fake.

There have been about 6,000 Bigfoot sightings in North America.

Real-World Connection

Jeison Orlando Rodriguez Hernandez isn't a Bigfoot. But he does have big feet! He has a world record. He has the biggest feet in the world. His feet are 16 inches (40.6 cm) long. His shoe size is 26. He has a hard time finding shoes. Since age 14, he has worn shoes made of cloth material. These shoes only last three weeks. Sometimes, he goes barefoot. He said, "I would look at other people and say, 'How I would like a little pair of shoes.'" Other kids bullied him. He saw a doctor. He has an overactive gland. The gland causes super growth. He's also really tall. He's 7 feet 3 inches (2.2 m) tall. He plays basketball. He wants to learn to bake. He wants to help depressed people.

Roger Patterson and Robert Gimlin went to Bluff Creek. They did this in 1967. They searched for Bigfoot. They wanted to make a film. They went into the forest. They filmed a female Bigfoot. They filmed her walking along the river.

Some people believed the film. Some people didn't. They thought the Bigfoot was someone in an ape suit. But special effects weren't good enough back then. Also, humans can't copy the Bigfoot's gait.

Real or not, Bigfoot fascinates.

The Patterson-Gimlin film is the most important piece of evidence for Bigfoot believers.

Did You Know?

- Native American tribes have over 60 different words for Bigfoot.

- Jane Goodall is a famous scientist. She's an expert on chimpanzees. She's interested in Bigfoot. She said, "Maybe they don't exist, but I want them to."

- Bigfoot was on the endangered species list. This happened in Russia, Germany, and France.

- Bigfoot aren't affected by pepper spray. They don't have allergies. They don't sneeze.

- Some people think Bigfoot are aliens.

- There are awards to find Bigfoot. One award is $10 million.

- *Sasquatch* comes from the word *sasq'ets*. It means "wild men." It's from the Halkomelem language. This language is spoken by some Native Americans.

- Chewbacca is a popular character in *Star Wars*. He was played by Peter Mayhew. He filmed in Northern California. He was in "Bigfoot country." Mayhew needed security. His security wore bright vests. He didn't want to be mistaken for Bigfoot. He didn't want to get shot.

- Some hair samples have been collected. Most samples are from known animals. But some are "origin unknown." The hair samples are more human than animal. Some people think this is Bigfoot proof.

- The only continent that doesn't have "wild men" stories is Antarctica.

Consider This!

Take a Position: Some people believe in Bigfoot. They believe people's sightings. They believe people's encounters. They believe the footprints. Some people don't believe in Bigfoot. There's no DNA evidence. There aren't any hair samples. There aren't any bones. Do you think Bigfoot are real or not? Argue your point with reasons and evidence.

Say What? Cultures have many stories about hairy humanlike creatures. Read 45th Parallel Press's book about werewolves. How are werewolves and Bigfoot similar? How are they different?

Think About It! Many people have pretended to see Bigfoot. They faked photos. They faked videos. One person made a Bigfoot. He used rubber, foam, and camel hair. He told people it was a Bigfoot. Why do you think people do this?

Learn More

* Bigfoot Field Researchers Organization: www.bfro.net
* Brockenbrough, Martha. *Finding Bigfoot: Everything You Need to Know*. New York: Feiwel and Friends, 2013.
* Michalak, Jamie, and Mark Fearing (illustrator). *So You Want to Catch a Bigfoot?* Somerville, MA: Candlewick Press, 2011.
* Theisen, Paul. *Bigfoot*. Minneapolis: Bellwether Media, 2011.

Glossary

abominable (uh-BAH-muh-nuh-buhl) horrible

gaits (GAYTS) walking styles

remains (rih-MAYNZ) dead body parts

ridge (RIJ) long bump

sightings (SITE-ingz) reports of people seeing things

soles (SOHLZ) the bottoms of feet

species (SPEE-sheez) groups of animal types

stalk (STAWK) to follow in a predatory manner

territorial (ter-ih-TOR-ee-uhl) protective of one's area

upright (UHP-rite) standing; in a vertical position

Index

About the Author

Dr. Virginia Loh-Hagan is an author, university professor, former classroom teacher, and curriculum designer. She has little feet. She can actually buy kids' shoes. She lives in San Diego with her very tall husband and very naughty dogs. To learn more about her, visit www.virginialoh.com.